ALL ACTION

KAYAKING

ALAN FOX

LERNER PUBLICATIONS COMPANY
MINNEAPOLIS

Titles in this series
Backpacking
Climbing
Kayaking
Mountain Biking
Skateboarding
Skiing
Survival Skills
Wind and Surf

Photographs are reproduced by permission of the following: p. 12, Brian and Cherry Alexander; p. 7 (top), Allsport/ Cirotteau-Lambolez; p. 10, Allsport/David Cannon; p. 17 (bottom), Allsport/G.Planchenault; p. 39, Allsport/Howard Boylan; p. 8, Eye Ubiquitous/Paul Prestidge; p. 9, Eye Ubiquitous/Thomas; p. 24, Eye Ubiquitous/David Higgs; p. 35, Eye Ubiquitous; pp. 6, 7 (bottom), 15, 18, 19, 20, 21, 22, 23 (both), 26, 27, 28, 29, 40, 41, 42, 43, 45, Alan Fox; p. 30, Tony Stone Worldwide/Tony Tickle; pp. 4, 25, 31, 32, 33, 34, 37, 38, Tony Tickle; pp. 5, 16, Topham/Leif R. Jansson; pp. 11, 36, ZEFA. Front cover photo by Tony Tickle. Back cover photo by Alan Fox. Artwork on page 13 by Brian Davey.

First published in the United States in 1993
by Lerner Publications Company

Copyright © 1992 by Wayland (Publishers) Limited
First published in 1992 by Wayland (Publishers) Ltd
61 Western Rd, Hove, East Sussex BN3 1JD, England

Library of Congress Cataloging-in-Publication Data
Fox, Alan, 1961-
     Kayaking / Alan Fox.
        p.   cm. — (All action)
     Includes bibliographical references (p.) and index.
     Summary: Discusses the equipment, techniques, competitions
and other aspects of kayaking.
        ISBN 0-8225-2482-1
        1. Kayaking—Juvenile literature. [1. Kayaking.]
     I. Title. II. Series
     GV783.F8 1993   92-5548
     797.1'22—dc20   CIP
                                             AC

Printed in Italy
Bound in the United States of America
1 2 3 4 5 6 7 8 9 10 02 01 00 99 98 97 96 95 94 93

Contents

INTRODUCTION

There are many different ways to kayak. You could paddle across a lake, enjoy a weeklong expedition on a river, or experience the thrill of **white-water** kayaking. Kayaking is a water sport that uses a special type of boat — a narrow, closed-decked canoe with one or more openings in the deck, where paddlers sit. Kayakers usually use a paddle with two blades, one on each end of a handle.

I learned to kayak in a youth group. Our adult leader was extremely enthusiastic about kayaking and taught us the basic skills on a local canal. As my confidence grew, I began to try new techniques, and eventually I dared to venture into faster-moving water. I capsized (flipped over) often, but I had already learned to bail out and swim — towing my boat along — to the shore. After quickly emptying the water from the kayak, I'd be back on the water again.

There were two advantages to learning with a youth group. The lessons gave us all exciting weekends away, and everyone started out with the same skills. It's tough to learn with people who are better than you, because watching them can make

you feel as though you'll never be as good.

Those weekend trips away gave me a real taste of adventure. We would head out of town late on Friday nights, packed into a rattling old van and towing a trailer stacked with kayaks. We would sleep in the loft of a farmer's barn. After eating a breakfast cooked up on old oil stoves, we would drive on to the river.

When we got there, we would all file out of the van and peer over the nearest bridge at the river below.

Don Starkell and his son, Dana, finished a 12,181-mile (19,600-km) canoe voyage in 1982. Starting in Winnipeg, Manitoba, their voyage took them south on the Red River, into the Mississippi River system, down to the Gulf of Mexico, around the east coast of Mexico and Central America, along the north coast of South America, and into the Orinoco, Negro, and Amazon rivers. They encountered sharks, crocodiles, piranhas, whales, and scorpions. Their voyage took them two years to complete.

Was the water level high or low? What would the **rapids** be like? Our enthusiasm was always high. In practically no time at all, we would carry our boats down to the water's edge. Alongside the kayaks, we'd put on warm clothes, life jackets, spray decks, and helmets. Our hearts would thump in anticipation. The tales we had heard of monster rapids eating kayakers whole could all come true in the next few hours.

I vividly remember the first rapid I ever paddled and the fear I felt before I reached it. The waves crashing down on the deck of my

kayak threatened to capsize me, but I survived. All the skills I had learned on flat water came to my aid, and my fear dissolved into excitement. I was hooked. Kayaking was a whole new world of adventure—one that I'm still enjoying.

My senses were tantalized as I tried all kinds of kayaking. There was the peaceful silence of calm, secluded rivers, the crashing turbulence of white water, the power of the sea and the surf, and the magnificent scenery of coastal cliffs and caves. I also enjoyed the thrill of competition — racing against the clock, avoiding slalom gates, and hearing spectators cheer. No matter what type of kayaking I tried, I made new friends and visited new places.

ABOVE

A kayaker punches through the rapids.

RIGHT

Kayakers can include waterfalls in their river descents, but they must follow proper precautions.

GETTING STARTED

Taking up a new sport on your own is pretty difficult. The best way to learn to kayak quickly and safely is to get expert help.

Many cities, schools, and colleges have kayak clubs. Local kayak clubs usually run some courses, from one-day introduction sessions to whole beginners' courses that might last a week. Many outdoors stores also advertise and sponsor these classes to develop new customers. One advantage of taking a course is that you will learn with people who have about the same ability as you do.

Your first lesson will cover the basics of kayaking. You will learn about equipment and proper clothing, techniques for steering the kayak, and essential safety precautions. One safety rule you should always remember is never to kayak with less than two other people. Additional lessons will improve your kayaking skills.

Most classes provide all the equipment you will need. However, you should wear suitable clothes. If your class is held during the summer months, wear shorts or thin running pants, a T-shirt and warm top, a pullover windbreaker, and sturdy tennis shoes. You are almost certain to capsize, so try to choose clothes

LEFT

Kayakers "raft up" as part of an introductory course.

made of fabrics that won't absorb water easily.

If the class is held in the spring or fall, wear a **wetsuit**. Most kayakers use a long john, which is a full-length, one-piece wetsuit without sleeves. Long johns won't restrict arm movement, which is essential for paddling. For even more protection from cold weather, wetsuit boots will keep your feet much warmer than wet tennis shoes will. If you plan on doing a lot of kayaking, you should get a paddling jacket or a waterproof pullover with a snug **neoprene** or rubber collar and cuffs.

Safety tips
- *Always wear a life jacket*
- *Wear a helmet on white-water rivers*
- *Wear sturdy footwear and carry spare warm clothes in a waterproof bag*
- *Know how to rescue yourself if you capsize*
- *Fill all spare room in the kayak with **buoyancy bags***
- *Never paddle alone*
- *Check prevailing weather conditions*
- *Check out the river in advance. Find out where you can put your kayak in and how difficult the paddling will be.*
- *Learn first-aid and resuscitation techniques*

RIGHT

If you take a kayaking class, you can try out the sport without having to buy all the equipment.

ABOVE

A group of kayakers practice rescue techniques.

Kayaking always involves some danger. To participate safely, you must be a good swimmer. Make sure you know the safety rules and can perform self-rescue techniques before you go on any trip.

Practice the **wet exit** — escaping an overturned kayak — in calm water until you are completely comfortable with the technique. To make a wet exit, release your **spray deck** (the waterproof skirting that you wear around your chest and abdomen and which forms a seal over the opening of the kayak) by pulling on the grab loop located at the front. Roll forward out of the kayak, push it aside, and swim to the surface. Then stay with your kayak.

The ultimate form of self-rescue is the **roll** — righting the kayak after it has overturned, without getting out. Rolling a kayak is easiest to learn in

Hazards to avoid on rivers
● *Overhanging trees on the outside of bends and trees submerged in the main flow*
● *Weirs (small dams built to regulate or redirect water flow) and low-head dams*
● *Moored craft and docks*
● *Fishing boats and swimmers*

ABOVE

A novice paddler listens to advice from her instructor during white-water training.

a class held in a swimming pool or in shallow, calm water. The maneuver, in which the paddler thrusts with the paddle while executing a hip snap, is especially valuable while kayaking on white water or in surf. In those waters, quickly rolling yourself upright means you have saved yourself from a long, potentially dangerous swim.

The only way to improve your kayaking skills is to practice. Books may help you to understand the finer points of maneuvers and paddle strokes, but they are not a substitute for actual experience. The more you paddle, the more confidence you will gain. What you do after your first lesson is up to you. With two-thirds of the world's surface covered in water, the possibilities are endless.

Over the top

Jessie Sharp of Nashville, Tennessee, tried kayaking the Horseshoe Falls, one of two waterfalls making up the Niagara Falls, in June 1990. Confident that he would succeed, he made dinner reservations for his planned celebration. However, the waterfall proved to be too powerful. Jessie's kayak was recovered at the bottom, but he didn't survive.

EQUIPMENT

Kayaking began with the Inuits (commonly called Eskimos) who live in some Arctic regions, including northern Canada, Greenland, Alaska, and the northeastern tip of Russia. Inuits built lightweight, wooden frames and covered them with sealskin or the skin of a caribou (a type of deer). An opening in the deck of this kayak was large enough to fit one person, who sat on the floor of it and paddled. Some kayaks were made with two holes, to seat two people. These early kayaks were used primarily for fishing and hunting.

Now used mainly for recreation, kayaks come in many different designs and sizes. For most activities, a general-purpose kayak is fine. However, if you plan to kayak in the ocean or enter races, you may need a kayak designed specifically for those activities.

The maneuverability of a kayak depends on its shape, length, and weight. A long kayak with a round hull, or bottom, is easy to paddle in a straight line. A short kayak with a flat hull is easy to turn, but more difficult to keep in a straight line. Kayaks with a lot of curve, called **rocker**, along the bottom from bow (front) to stern (back), are easier to turn than kayaks

RIGHT

Kayaks built by Inuits were the forerunners of modern kayaks.

12

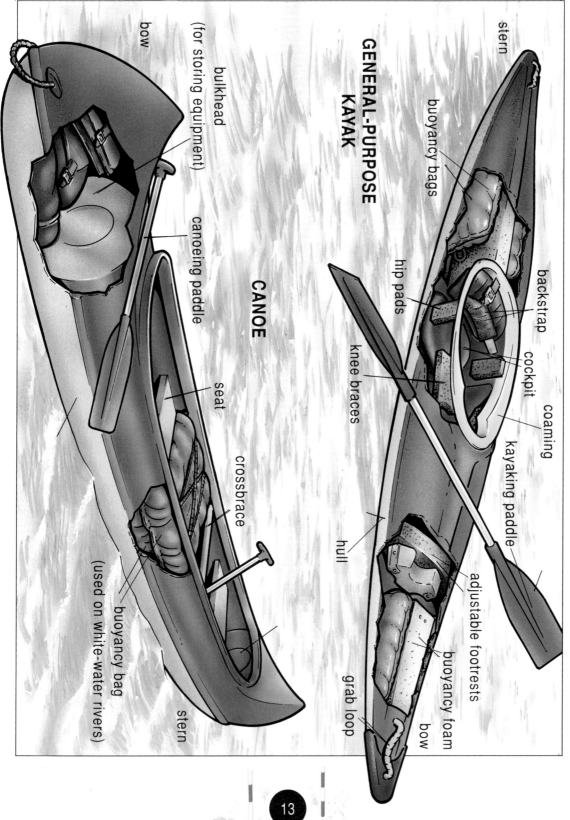

GENERAL-PURPOSE KAYAK

stern

buoyancy bags

hip pads

knee braces

hull

backstrap

cockpit

coaming

kayaking paddle

adjustable footrests

buoyancy foam

bow

grab loop

CANOE

bow

bulkhead
(for storing equipment)

canoeing paddle

seat

crossbrace

buoyancy bag
(used on white-water rivers)

stern

without much rocker. General-purpose kayaks are a compromise. They travel well in a straight line and are not too hard to turn.

There are many different types of kayaks to choose from. Before you buy one, you should try out as many as you can to see which type you prefer. In addition to the type and its cost, consider the materials. Plastic is lightweight, less likely to get damaged by rocks, and is virtually maintenance-free.

Any kayak you choose should have several safety features. These include strong **grab loops**, adjustable footrests, and enough internal **buoyancy** — floatation — to keep the kayak afloat if it takes in water.

Touring kayaks are longer than general-purpose kayaks. Touring kayaks come in one- or two-person versions and are ideal for daylong outings or long-distance trips on rivers and lakes. If you use a spray deck, touring kayaks are fine for easy white water, and they usually have enough space to store camping equipment and supplies for overnight trips. Some touring kayaks have large, open **cockpits**.

General-purpose kayaks are suitable for most white-water rivers. However, as the popularity of white-water kayaking grew, manufacturers began constructing kayaks for certain types of rivers. Some are designed for long wilderness trips, and others were developed specially for narrow mountain rivers that require a lot of technical skill.

White-water kayaks are often rated by their volume (the amount of air enclosed by the shell) and their length. High-volume kayaks provide greater stability in white water. They are often used on expeditions, mainly because they provide ample storage space.

General-purpose kayaks fall into the medium-volume category and are excellent for beginners. They are adequate for most kayaking adventures. Low-volume kayaks are usually those designed for competitive slalom or freestyle kayaking (which involves doing acrobatic stunts).

The length of a kayak affects its ability to turn. On mountain rivers (which are often narrow and steep), being able to turn quickly is essential, so many short kayaks have been developed. These kayaks frequently

have rounded ends to keep them from catching on rocks. They have almost the same volume as a general-purpose kayak.

In addition to a kayak, you will need a paddle, life jacket, spray deck, and helmet (which you should wear when you are learning and whenever you go white-water kayaking).

Like kayaks, paddles come in a wide variety of styles and are made from different materials. The blades on kayak paddles are usually **feathered** — that is, they are set at 90-degree angles to each other. Feathering the blades reduces the drag, or wind resistance, of the upper blade as it slices through the air while the lower one is being pulled through the water. Choose the correct size paddle by standing it upright and reaching up to the top blade. If you can just curl your fingers over the top of the blade, then the paddle should be the right length for you.

Paddles can be simple plywood blades on an aluminum shaft; hand-crafted, all-wooden paddles; or high-tech fiberglass, resin, and aluminum paddles designed for the roughest

The Mike Jones Rally, which attracts around 2,000 paddlers annually, holds one of the more bizarre races in canoeing — The Cardboard Canoe Race. Strict rules allow no serious entries. Fancy dress and theme boats are the order of the day, and canoes must be constructed only from cardboard and tape. Many of the entries sink or capsize before they reach the finish line.

ABOVE

Kayaking requires specialized equipment for the most enjoyable — and the safest — outings.

use. Most blades are curved to help the kayaker get the most power from every stroke.

A life jacket is the most important piece of equipment you will buy. It will keep you afloat if you capsize and become separated from your kayak. It will also cushion you from rocks in white water or ocean surfs. Your life jacket should allow you to move your arms freely. Choose one that fits snugly, but comfortably. Life jackets for expedition or white-water paddling will often have extra buoyancy to keep your head well out of the water. They may also have pockets for storing equipment (such as flares and a first-aid kit) and a built-in safety harness for rescues.

S pray decks will keep water out of the kayak. They are usually made from waterproof nylon or neoprene and are designed to form a seal between you and the kayak. A spray deck fits snugly around your midsection and attaches to the

kayak's **coaming** (the rim around the cockpit). Make sure the spray deck you use has a strong release loop, so that you can pull it off the cockpit quickly and easily in an emergency.

You should always wear a helmet when paddling on shallow rocky rivers and white water. If you capsize, your head will be the closest thing to the rocks below the water surface. Find a helmet that fits comfortably and snugly. Make sure it covers your forehead.

The variety of equipment available can be bewildering. If you aren't sure what to get, ask an expert for help.

ABOVE

Ready to go. Two kayakers pause for a photo before heading back onto the river.

RIGHT

Room for two! The front storage compartment of this kayak has many uses.

RIVER ADVENTURE

At breakfast we studied the maps, checking the terrain of the surrounding country and looking for roads or tracks that would take us farther upstream to begin our day's kayaking.

"How far?" someone asked.

"It's about 40 kilometers (about 25 miles) with only a few small rapids," I said.

All we had to do was to get there.

Although we had to drive only 30 miles (50 km), it would take a couple of hours to get to our starting point. There were few roads — only dirt tracks and the added hazard of wild animals. We were in the African bush near the banks of the Zambezi River.

After being cramped in an old Land Rover for two hours, with seven kayaks strapped on the roof, we finally reached the put-in point. The day's

journey would take between four and seven hours, depending on the speed of the river and how fast we paddled.

A wide expanse of water lay ahead of us. On either side were the palm-fringed, sandy banks of the river. Baboons skipped from branch to branch in the trees. One moment they were still and watchful. The next moment, they were scurrying and screeching. Antelope, drinking at the river's edge, sensed our intrusion and sprang away into the trees. Only the large kudu antelope stood firm, eyeing us suspiciously as we started our voyage.

Coming around a bend in the river, we were faced with three large elephants standing in the shallow waters. Cautiously we edged away from them, not wanting to get caught under their feet.

There were a few small rapids in this section of the river, but they were all very easy to navigate. The runs traveled straight along in well-defined channels. The only real hazards were the hippos and crocodiles that lived in the river.

Every so often we banged on the decks of our kayaks. At the noise, the hippos, who grazed on the riverbed, would rise to the surface — giving us enough time to avoid them.

Crocodiles often float with only their snouts on the surface of the water, so they are difficult to spot. They lurk in still waters. For every crocodile we saw, we knew that there were others that we didn't see.

As we neared the end of the trip, we began to pass small villages. Canoes carved from tree trunks lay idle on the banks, providing a stark contrast to our colorful, high-tech, plastic kayaks.

BELOW

High-spirited kayakers surf the "Thunder Waves" on the Zambezi River.

We found a
unique way to
transport a kayak
in Nepal's
Kathmandu.

Our trip down the Zambezi River was a very special adventure, and the sense of excitement I felt on that day was similar to my first explorations of the rivers and canals around my home and the weekend trips I took with the youth group.

Day trips are the easiest trips you

can organize. They can be anywhere from a few to 25 miles (40 km), depending on water conditions. In slow-moving rivers or streams, you may travel at a rate of only 2 miles an hour (about 3 km/h). On a river that is flowing faster, your speed may double. Speed is not really important. Take time to explore side streams, creeks, and backwaters, and keep an eye out for wildlife.

Before taking any trip in the wilderness, follow these precautions:

- Plan your route and tell someone where you are going.
- Always have at least three people in your group.
- Wear the right clothes for the weather conditions, and carry spare warm clothes in a waterproof bag.
- Take along food (in a waterproof bag) and drinking water.
- Ask an experienced person to go with you.

Before you plan your own adventure with friends, make sure you have plenty of experience in kayaking. Multi-day trips, or touring, require detailed preparation, mainly

BELOW

Kayakers pack their boats before a descent of the Modi Khola River in Nepal.

because you need to carry the right amount of camping gear, food, and water. You can start with a single overnight trip to gain experience, then work up to multi-day trips.

Stow your equipment so the weight is evenly distributed throughout the kayak. If you put all the heavy items in the back or to one side, your kayak will be harder to maneuver. Equally important, always pack your clothes and food in watertight bags or containers. If you capsize, they will protect your gear from the water.

Many people cut down on weight by using **survival bags**—lightweight, waterproof sleeping bags — instead of tents and by carrying dehydrated (dried) food. After a few trips, you will know what equipment suits you best.

ABOVE

Exploring a river near your home can be a real adventure.

RIGHT

You should prepare carefully for multi-day trips.

The roar of breaking waves crashing upon one another as they head toward shore is enough to beckon a surfer into the water. On warm holiday weekends, the sea is packed with swimmers and surfers, all occupying a small area close to the shore. Beyond them, the clear blue ocean stretches to the horizon, disappearing out of sight around the headlands on either side. This is the territory of the sea kayaker, away from the crowds, exploring rocky coastlines and secluded beaches. Oftentimes, the only way to reach these places is from the sea. The kayaker can paddle beneath the rock arches that waves have eroded and skim quietly into dark caves.

The sea provides kayakers and canoeists with an endless range of adventures. You can go on short trips along the coast, visit nearby islands, or undertake lengthy sea voyages.

A general-purpose kayak is suitable for a day trip, but special sea kayaks are better for longer journeys in the ocean. Sea kayaks are long and narrow, designed to cut through waves and cover long distances. Compartments in the bow and stern are sealed, and there are watertight hatches on the deck. The air trapped in these places makes the kayak virtually unsinkable and provides dry storage areas for equipment. Deck lines — ropes attached to the top of the kayak — hold equipment the

ABOVE

Surfing on a highly maneuverable wave ski is thrilling.

LEFT

A group of sea kayakers pass between cliffs and rocks. Note the long, thin shape of the sea kayak and the deck hatches in front and back.

paddler might need while traveling, such as spare paddles and maps.

Having the right kayak is only one part of a successful adventure. Sea kayaking demands a knowledge of weather patterns and tidal streams, as well as good **navigation** skills. At sea the weather can change suddenly, and you must be prepared to escape dangerous conditions.

Some kayakers stay near the beach with the surfers and swimmers. Surf kayakers head for the big waves so they can ride in on them, much like surfers do on their surfboards. If the waves are about to break on top of you, you have two options: you can do a loop or go for a bongo slide. Loops are done by slowing down as the wave breaks. The wave will then pick up the back of the boat, the front will drive down, and the boat will go end over end and pop up on the back side of the wave. A bongo slide is done by bracing sideways on the wave as it carries you in (while doing this you should keep an eye out for anyone in your way). If a collision is likely, do a roll and the wave will pass you by.

Many surf kayakers use special kayaks, such as surf skis (which are flat-bottomed) and wave skis (which are similar to surfboards, except that you sit on them and use paddles). Both handle like surfboards, but they pick up the waves sooner.

WHITE WATER

After a week of practice on some Alpine rivers, we drove to Austria to attempt the River Isel. The guidebook listed the river at class 5, so we knew that we would be in for some hard white-water kayaking.

At each bend there were stretches of white water lasting several hundred yards. We could see how the river had earned its reputation. At river level, the sight was breathtaking. The thundering water, crashing through a jumble of giant boulders, would give us few places to stop. All of us were nervous as we inspected possible routes down the first major rapid. After 10 minutes of discussion, we scrambled back to our kayaks.

With spray decks on, helmets buckled, and life jackets secured, we pushed off. The speed of the water was exhilarating, and the 100 yards or so to the first breakout (calmer water) passed in seconds. The main hazard, a large waterfall, was next.

I had little time to prepare, but I was still on the correct line, or route. I paddled hard into the drop, using all

LEFT

A kayaker heads into a tricky rapid.

RIGHT

Coming out of a large drop — the force of the water on the back deck almost stands the kayak on end.

River ratings

Sections of white-water rivers are rated according to their difficulty. Ratings given in river guides may change, depending on river levels, recent rock slides, or fallen trees.

Class 1:   *Easy — occasional small rapids with few or no obstacles.*

Class 2:   *Moderate — small rapids and waves that are easy to get across.*

Class 3:   *Difficult — rapids with hazards and irregular waves that should be scouted from shore ahead of time. Kayakers will have to do some complex maneuvering to avoid obstacles.*

Class 4:   *Very difficult — long, large rapids and falls with dangerous hazards that must be scouted from shore beforehand. Kayakers will have to execute precise maneuvers, including rolls. Rescues will be difficult.*

Class 5:   *Extremely difficult — violent rapids and falls with narrow routes and lots of dangerous hazards. Only kayakers with expert skills should attempt these sections, and rescuers should be stationed downriver in case of a mishap.*

Class 6:   *Nearly impossible — the route will be extremely difficult to find. These sections should be attempted only by teams of expert kayakers following all precautions.*

The wildest rivers

Walt Blackadar pioneered big water kayaking in the United States. His attempt on Alaska's Susitna River almost ended in catastrophe when he capsized and was forced to swim in the powerful rapids. He was rescued by a waiting helicopter and returned the next day to conquer the river without mishap.

*The Susitna River was regarded by many paddlers as the wildest in the world, until a team of U.S. kayakers, led by Rob Lesser of Idaho, made the first **descent** of the Stikine River in British Columbia, Canada. The fearsome rapids deep in the bottom of an almost inaccessible canyon led many people to declare this river nearly impossible to kayak.*

my strength to punch through the **stopper**—a circulating undercurrent that sometimes holds kayaks in one place. The water crashed all around, and I pulled hard on the paddle. Daylight again . . . I was through. But there was no time to relax. More rapids lay ahead! I glanced back quickly to see Richard pulling through the fall, with Guy following close behind him. We had all done well, and most importantly, we were safe.

You should try running class 5 white water like the section I traveled on the River Isel only after you have practiced a lot on the white water of lower grade rivers. Not every kayaker enjoys paddling through this type of white water. Many people prefer to challenge themselves on longer, easier rapids, where mistakes are unlikely to be life-threatening.

Kayakers usually tackle long sets of rapids in sections. They use **eddies** — the calm water behind rocks and other river obstructions — to rest and look over the next section of the rapids. Some kayakers also paddle upstream from eddy to eddy, in a technique known as **eddy hopping**, to ride down the rapids again.

If you're not sure what's down-stream, you will have to head for the bank and get out to inspect the river. A thin horizon line ahead may signal a waterfall. You should always be careful when descending waterfalls, because there may be hazards in the pools below.

A kayaker descends a big waterfall along the River Rizzanese on the French island of Corsica. Running falls of this size requires years of experience and expert skills.

COMPETITION

You must have determination and be in good physical shape to succeed in competition. Skill and experience, as well as having the right equipment, are also extremely important.

However, you don't need to be of World Championship caliber to enjoy competitions. All kayaking events are fun to enter, and various levels of competition have been created so that people of all ages and abilities can participate.

Gompetitions attract a lot of spectators and competitors. More often than not, a weekend slalom or

RIGHT

In slalom racing, the competitors must negotiate a number of gates on a winding course.

LEFT

The look of concentration is evident on this slalom kayaker's face as he heads toward the next gate.

racing event turns into a large social gathering, where people make new friends who share a love for kayaking.

S lalom racing is the ultimate test of fitness, ability to read the water, and the skill to control a kayak. Each competitor paddles a short course of white water, through numbered gates. A slalom gate is two poles suspended over the water. Competitors must go through green gates while traveling downstream and red gates while traveling upstream. If any part of a competitor's paddle, boat, or body touches the poles, time penalties are added. The paddler with the fastest time out of two runs wins.

Slalom kayaks have changed over the years. The earliest designs were similar to modern high-volume kayaks, but kayakers eventually began using low-volume boats with nearly flat decks. These kayaks can slip under slalom poles more easily than high-volume boats, which helps competitors avoid penalties.

Entering a slalom event will not only give you a chance to compete, but it will also help you perfect your paddling skills.

Richard Fox

Richard Fox of England had already won the World Slalom Championships three times. During the 1987 World Championships at Bourg, France, everyone wondered if Fox could win the title for an unprecedented fourth time.

Fox's first run of the competition was the fastest of the whole World Championships, but a penalty on gate 13 left him in second place. On his second run, he also produced a fast time, but again he was unlucky at gate 13 when the tip of his kayak touched a pole. Fox slipped to fourth place behind the new world champ, Anton Prijon of Germany.

Many people thought that Fox's long reign had come to an end, but in the 1989 World Championships on the Savage River in Maryland, he took them by surprise. Although his second run began with a penalty on gate 1, he moved into overdrive, taking 2.47 seconds off his previous run, enough to give him a substantial lead for his fourth World Championship win. Fox proved that he is perhaps the greatest slalom paddler of all time.

Wild-water racing is demanding, not only physically but also mentally. A wild-water race is usually held over a river course between 2 and 15 miles (3 to 25 km) long with at least class 3 rapids. Kayakers must "read the water" accurately and find the best route through the rapids quickly in order to log the fastest time. A bad route, a rock hit, or a capsize will cause a competitor to lose vital seconds.

Wild-water racing kayaks are designed for maximum forward speed through rapids. The kayaks have virtually no rocker, but a V-shaped hull helps the kayak cut through the waves. A wedge-shaped section

A double kayak plunges into a fall during river competition.

behind the cockpit gives the kayak an even more distinctive look.

Competitors start at least 30 seconds apart, with a 5-second countdown to the start. From then on, every stroke counts. If a kayaker is caught by a person who started later, he or she must move aside for the faster paddler or face disqualification.

BELOW

Marathon paddlers portage their kayak around an obstacle during a race.

The word "marathon" is usually associated with the long-distance running event. Kayak marathons are, fortunately, much shorter. Races range from about 3 or 4 miles (about 5 or 7 km) in the lower divisions to 12 miles (20 km) or more in the top divisions. Kayaking in marathon races often involves getting past obstacles such as locks, dams, and rapids. Sometimes the only way around these obstacles is to **portage** — that is, to carry the kayak around the obstacle.

Most marathons have a group start, in which all the competitors line up together and begin paddling at the same time. The person who gets to

The 125-mile (200-km) race between Devizes and Westminster in England is one of the toughest nonstop races in the world. Winning times are under 16 hours, but many competitors aim to complete the race within 24 hours.

The Arctic Canoe Race starts more than 250 miles (400 km) north of the Arctic Circle at Kilpisjarvi, Finland, close to the point where the borders of Sweden, Norway, and Finland meet. The race covers 334 miles (537 km) and lasts for about six days.

the front of the pack has an advantage at the first portage.

Races are held at national and local levels. Many kayaking clubs organize their own mini-marathon series. In most club races, competitors do not have special marathon kayaks. The emphasis is on taking part rather than winning. These events are a good way for you to get in shape, while you try to improve your best time over a set course.

Special marathon kayaks are long and narrow. They seem quite unstable

Molokai Hoe canoe race

The Molokai Hoe outrigger canoe race is run between the Hawaiian islands of Oahu and Molokai, a distance of 40 miles (64 km). The race has been held every year since 1952 and commemorates the invasion of Oahu in 1795 by the Hawaiian chief Kamahameka. After crossing the Kaiwi Channel with a fleet of war canoes, Kamahameka defeated the rival warriors. The outrigger canoes are up to 46 feet (14 m) long. Three of the six paddlers are replaced every 15 minutes by fresh paddlers, who board the passing boat from the water.

at first. However, like bicycles, they become more stable when they're moving. Marathon kayaks usually are steered with a foot-operated **rudder** so the kayaker can maintain maximum forward paddling power at all times.

Sprint races are relatively short, extremely fast, flatwater competitions. Racers generally line up in individual lanes at the start and race over straight courses. Distances for international and Olympic events are 500 and 1,000 meters. The annual World Championships also include a 10,000-meter, long-distance race.

Another popular sprint-racing event is Dragon Boat racing. This spectacular race involves canoes up to 40 feet (12 m) long, crewed by a team of 20 paddlers. A drummer in the boat beats a rhythm to help the crew paddle together.

In kayak polo, two teams of between two and five kayakers compete. They try to score goals by throwing a water polo ball at square goals suspended six feet (two m) above the water at both ends of a pool. Players are allowed to pass the ball by throwing it or by flicking it with the paddle. They can only hold the ball for five seconds, then they have to shoot it or pass it off. The other team gets the ball if a player is judged to have misused a paddle, barged into an opponent, or knocked the ball out of play. Capsizing an opponent is allowed, but only if he or she has the ball. Most players capsize, and they must be good at rolling if they want to get back into the game quickly.

While you can play kayak polo with general-purpose kayaks, manufacturers sell polo kayaks — also called bat boats. These kayaks are short with rounded ends. Many players wear face masks to protect themselves from others' paddles.

PLAYBOATING

Playboating, or play paddling, is freestyle kayaking — using rapids to perform acrobatics with a kayak. The sport is full of action and extreme maneuvers requiring a high degree of skill.

Before trying any freestyle maneuvers, you must be very good at rolling yourself upright after a capsize. To begin, all you need is a small stopper or a large wave that will help you perform basic tricks. Good freestylers can do maneuvers like front enders, in which the nose of the kayak is submerged and the kayak appears to be standing in water; popouts, which are like enders, except that the kayak actually becomes

airborne; and skyrockets, in which the kayak appears to squirt out of a stopper. Of course, these maneuvers are just the beginning. The best freestylers do them to set up stunts that are much harder to execute.

Playboaters also do numerous tricks with their paddles, such as throwing them into the air and catching them while balancing on a wave. The latest movement in freestyling is to perform stunts without using a paddle. The real experts can juggle oranges while surfing on a wave!

White-water "rodeos," which were first held in the United States, are now organized worldwide. These

ABOVE

A kayaker performs a popout and paddle twirl during a rodeo competition.

LEFT

A competitor surfs on a wave during the Rodeo World Championships.

Rodeo World Championships

The first World Rodeo Championship was held in 1990 off the coast of South Wales. The overall winner, and the first world champion, was Jan Kellner of Augsburg, Germany. Part of the skills heat involved a 26-foot (eight-m) seal launch off a cliff. Those who refused to try were assessed penalty points.

rodeos feature different kayaking events, such as wave surfing, stopper riding, and sprints. Judges award points for style, technique, and sheer courage. If you can smile while performing your tricks, you're bound to get additional bonus points.

As your kayaking skills develop, you will find plenty of opportunities to practice various freestyle maneuvers. The thrill of performing acrobatics will set your pulse racing. In addition to providing you with hours of fun, playboating will help you perfect your techniques and increase your confidence in extreme white-water rivers.

The most extreme playboats are squirtboats. These are very low-volume kayaks that are custom-built for each paddler. They just barely float on the surface of the water. Squirtboats have a very flat, thin bow and stern that help the kayaker execute very complex and radical moves. Squirtboat moves have names such as blasting, rocksplats, meltdowns, black attacks, and cartwheels. Learning each move can take hours, and perfecting them takes even more time.

EXPEDITIONS

Most of the work that goes into a kayaking expedition happens before any of the kayaks enter the water. You must plan carefully, otherwise you may find yourself in serious trouble far from any help. Only after considering all the details can you truly enjoy the challenge of a remote river adventure.

On our arrival in Lima, the capital of Peru, we rented a small bus to take us, our kayaks, and our equipment south along the Pan American Highway. We squeezed the kayaks into the bus, which had no roof rack, but then there was little room for anyone to sit. After 24 hours of nonstop driving in the cramped bus, we arrived in the small village of Haumbo, in the coastal mountains of southern Peru.

Four months of planning had gotten us this far. We had obtained sponsors (people willing to help pay for a venture) and made the necessary arrangements to transport ourselves and our gear to South America. We had drawn up lists of food and supplies to make sure we were properly equipped. The only thing left was to reach the Rio (River) Colca at the bottom of the Colca Canyon.

There are no roads going down into what is regarded as the world's deepest canyon. We would have to travel along a narrow, rough mule path. Armed with a phrase book of Latin-American Spanish, we entered

ABOVE

We loaded the kayaks onto mules at the start of our expedition.

LEFT

At Lima in Peru, our kayaks were squeezed into a bus, leaving little space for us!

Colca Canyon

A team of Polish residents was the first to descend the Rio Colca in the Colca Canyon of Peru. The team attempted the entire length of the canyon in May 1981, an expedition that took nearly a month to complete. The first 27 miles (44 km) from Cabanaconde to Canco took 11 days. It was a section they described as a combination of kayaking and mountaineering.

the only shop in the village. *"¿Donde puedo encontrar tres burros, por favor?"* we asked. The shop owner understood our request for three mules, which would transport our kayaks into the canyon. The following morning, we strapped the kayaks onto the mules' backs and trooped into the depths of the Colca Canyon.

T he eight-hour walk in was long and hot. In many places, the path crossed dangerous slopes of rock fragments. One slip would have sent us sliding hundreds of yards down. We reached the river with just enough time to find firewood before darkness fell.

During the night, we often heard the rumbling noise of rocks falling nearby. We had been warned that rockfalls were one of the hazards in the canyon, and we wondered if we should wear our helmets while sleeping. At the first light, we crawled from our survival bags, relit the fire, and began packing our kayaks for the three-day river journey ahead. Food, clothing, and other equipment went into tough waterproof bags that were secured inside the kayaks. Even after leaving behind all but the most essential equipment, we still managed to fill all the available space in the boats.

Within a couple of hours, we were

42

ABOVE

At last, we were on the river.

ready to paddle. We knew that there would be no turning back after we started — it would be virtually impossible to walk out of the canyon until we reached the end. Even so, we looked forward to the rapids ahead and the remote wilderness scenery that the canyon would offer.

We edged out into the fast-flowing water and headed into the first rapid of the day. The best part of our expedition, the river descent, had finally begun.

ACCESS

As your enthusiasm for kayaking grows, you will want to try your skills on different waterways. The land alongside many rivers is privately owned, and while some rivers have public access areas, others do not. If you cannot find a public access, you must get permission from a landowner to launch your kayaks. Other rivers may be protected from overuse, and a government agency may require you to obtain a wilderness-use permit before you embark on a kayaking trip.

Access agreements have arisen from conflicts between river users, such as anglers and kayakers. The best agreements will allow all users reasonable access to pursue their sport. You must find out beforehand if the river you plan to use has such an agreement in force. Ignoring it will give kayakers a bad name and could lead to a complete ban on kayaking.

On small mountain rivers, there isn't enough room for large groups. Keep the number of people in your group low, even if you have to split into subgroups and stagger your starting times.

Minor things such as being too noisy can offend local people. Be considerate of others who are using

---

Health precautions

Natural waterways, while appearing clean, contain many micro-organisms. The risk of contracting illness is small, but you should take some sensible precautions. Cover cuts before getting in the water, avoid drinking untreated water, and wash up in clean water after you have finished kayaking.

Blue-green algae, although naturally present in most water, will produce scum on the water surface under certain conditions. This scum is particularly noticeable along the edges of lakes after long periods of hot weather. The algae can be toxic, so avoid touching it. If you come into contact with it accidentally, wash it off as soon as possible.

If you become sick within two weeks after being in a river or lake, tell your doctor that you have been in contact with untreated water, especially if you have swallowed some. The information may help in diagnosis of your condition.

the river, and try to minimize your impact on the environment.

Kayaking and canoeing are environment-safe sports. Because they don't add to air or water pollution or create mechanical noise, kayaks and canoes are ideal for exploring wilderness areas and observing wildlife at close range. The shallowness of the boat ensures that life below the surface of the river will not be disturbed. Even high-action events like slalom, river racing, or long-distance competitions, do not damage sensitive environments.

Glossary

Access agreements   Plans developed by various water sport participants to allow fair use of a waterway by all the people who want to use it. Kayakers may be allowed on a river during certain times of the year, fishing enthusiasts during another time of year, and swimmers in a specified area during those same times.

Buoyancy   The ability to float

Buoyancy bags   Inflatable bags that fit underneath the deck of a kayak, trapping air that can't be displaced by water, to make the boat virtually unsinkable

Coaming   The rim around the cockpit, to which the spray deck is attached

Cockpit   The area of a kayak where you sit; the opening in the deck

Descent   A kayaking term that refers to a trip downstream, as on a river

Eddies   Areas of relatively calm water, found behind rocks and other obstacles that break the flow of water

Eddy hopping   A technique for paddling upstream, from eddy to eddy, to lessen the battle against the current

Feathered   The way kayak blades are set at 90-degree angles to one another. If the paddle were set on a flat surface, one blade would be flat on the surface, while the other would be perpendicular, or straight up and down, to the surface.

Grab loops   Cords of rope or nylon webbing fastened to both ends of a kayak and used for many purposes, including towing and docking the kayak

Navigation   The science of finding one's way on water

Neoprene   A cellular rubber material used to make wetsuits and spray decks. It has good insulating properties.

Portage   To carry a canoe or kayak across land in order to get from one body of water to another or to get around an impassable section of water

Rapids   Extremely fast-flowing sections of a river, characterized by white water and usually caused by terrain features beneath the surface of the water

Roll   Any of various methods by which you can right yourself and your kayak after a capsize without assistance and without leaving the kayak

Rocker   The amount of curvature, from bow to stern, on the bottom of a kayak. The rocker has a direct bearing on how easily the kayak turns or tracks along a straight line.

Rudder   A flat device attached to the rear of a kayak to help steer it; used primarily on touring or marathon kayaks

Spray deck   A piece of waterproof material that forms a seal between a kayaker's body and the opening of a kayak. Spray decks fit tightly over the torso and attach to the kayak so water can't get into the cockpit.

Stopper A circulating undercurrent that sometimes forms in river rapids. A kayak that gets caught in a stopper will have to fight the opposing forces of the stopper, which is pushing the kayak backward, and the rapids, which are pushing the kayak forward.

Survival bags A lightweight, waterproof bag that can fit over a sleeping bag to keep it dry. Survival bags can also be used alone, in an emergency, to keep someone warm. They can also be used alone, as sleeping bags, when the weather is sure to be quite warm.

Wet exit A method of escaping an overturned kayak. Wet exits involve releasing the spray deck from the kayak, rolling forward out of the kayak, and pushing the kayak out of the way so you can get to the surface.

Wetsuit An article of clothing that is designed to keep you warm in cold water. Wetsuits come in all styles, sizes, and colors. They are usually made of a fabric that allows water to pass through to your skin, but which provides a great deal of insulation to trap your body heat.

White water Rushing, foaming water found in rapids; caused by fast-flowing water that meets resistance beneath the water surface

Books

Dowd, John. *Sea Kayaking*. Seattle, Washington: University of Washington Press, 1988.

Harrison, Dave. *Sports Illustrated Canoeing*. New York, New York: Winner's Circle Books, 1988.

Kallner, Bill, and Donna Jackson. *Kayaking Whitewater*. Merrillville, Indiana: ICS Books, 1990.

O'Connor, Cameron, and John Lazenby. *First Descents: In Search of Wild Rivers*. Birmingham, Alabama: Menasha Ridge Press, 1989.

Videos

Introduction to Canoeing. Minneapolis, Minnesota: Quality Video, 1990.

A Second Helping: A Review of Kayaking Basics. Bryson City, North Carolina: Nantahala Outdoor Center, 1987.

More information

American Canoe Association
P.O. Box 1190
Newington, Virginia 22122
703-451-0141

Index